Adventures in Music

Book Four

Roy Bennett

CAMBRIDGE
UNIVERSITY PRESS

The orchestra

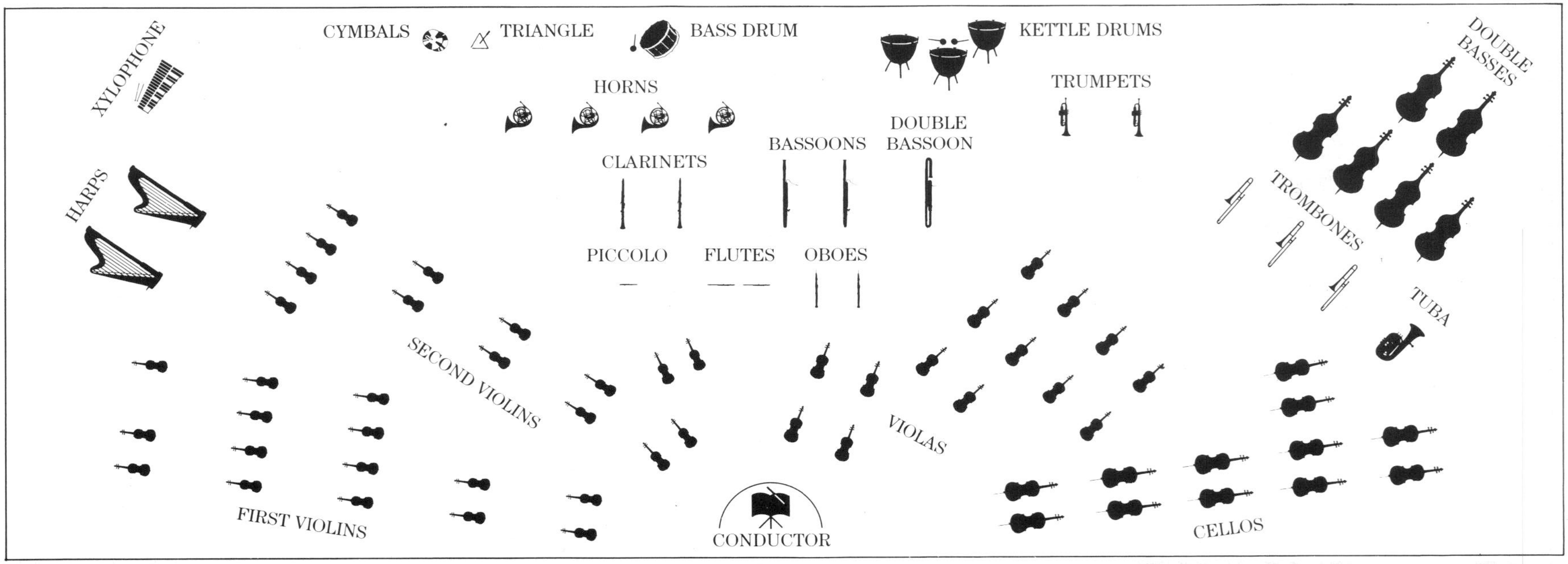

CYMBALS

TRIANGLE

BASS DRUM

KETTLE DRUMS

HORNS

CLARINETS

BASSOONS

DOUBLE BASSOON

TRUMPETS

TROMBONES

TUBA

DOUBLE BASSES

PICCOLO

FLUTES

OBOES

CELLOS

VIOLAS

CONDUCTOR

SECOND VIOLINS

FIRST VIOLINS

XYLOPHONE

HARPS

Sheep may safely graze

Johann Sebastian BACH
1685–1750
GERMANY

Sheep may safely graze is one of Bach's most famous pieces. He wrote this music when he was employed at the court of the Duke of Weimar. One of the Duke's friends (another Duke) was arranging a hunting party to celebrate his birthday. The Duke of Weimar was invited, and he asked Bach to write some music for the occasion. *Sheep may safely graze* was one of the pieces which Bach composed. It was performed after the hunt, at the Duke's birthday feast.

The composer of *Sheep may safely graze*

Bach was born in Germany in 1685 (the same year that Handel was born). He belonged to a very large and very musical family.

Bach never left Germany, and so he never became really famous during his lifetime. But he did move from town to town.

Sometimes he took the job of church organist and choir-master. Sometimes he became director of music at the court of a rich nobleman. In each of these jobs, Bach was expected to train musicians, and also to compose a great deal of music of all kinds for them to perform.

Bach married twice. His two wives between them gave him 20 children. Several of these became famous as composers or performers.

Listen to Bach's piece called *Sheep may safely graze*. Bach wrote this music as a song – to be sung by a soprano, accompanied by just a few instruments. But you will hear the music in a version for orchestra, made a few years ago by the English composer William Walton.

You will find Bach's tunes on the chart on the next page. Follow the chart as you listen to *Sheep may safely graze*.

Sheep may safely graze

1 The first tune, which sounds rather like a tune that shepherds might play on their pipes, is shared between clarinets and flutes.

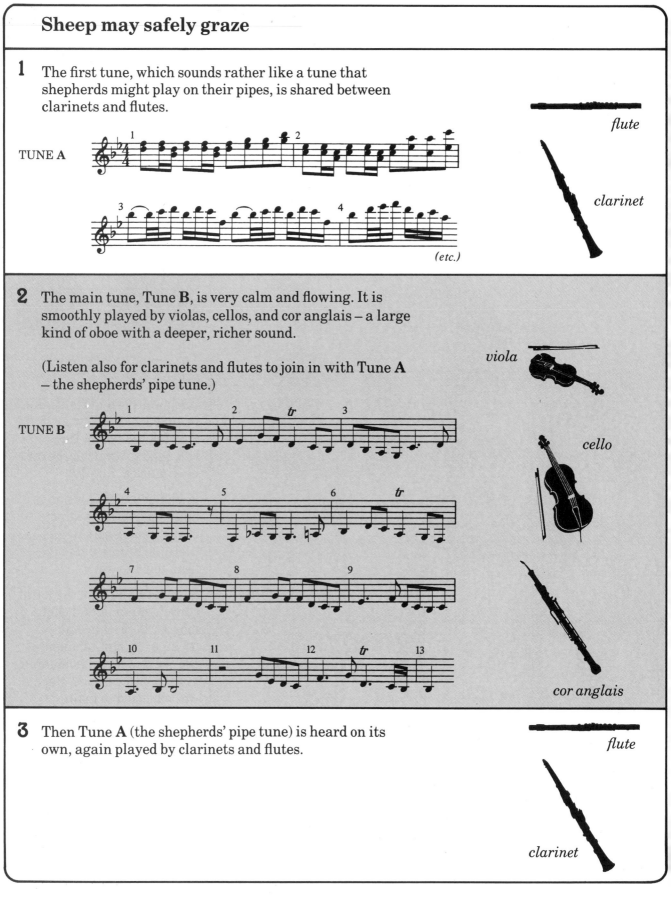

flute

clarinet

TUNE **A**

2 The main tune, Tune **B**, is very calm and flowing. It is smoothly played by violas, cellos, and cor anglais – a large kind of oboe with a deeper, richer sound.

(Listen also for clarinets and flutes to join in with Tune **A** – the shepherds' pipe tune.)

viola

cello

TUNE **B**

cor anglais

3 Then Tune **A** (the shepherds' pipe tune) is heard on its own, again played by clarinets and flutes.

flute

clarinet

4 The next tune is played by an oboe.

TUNE C

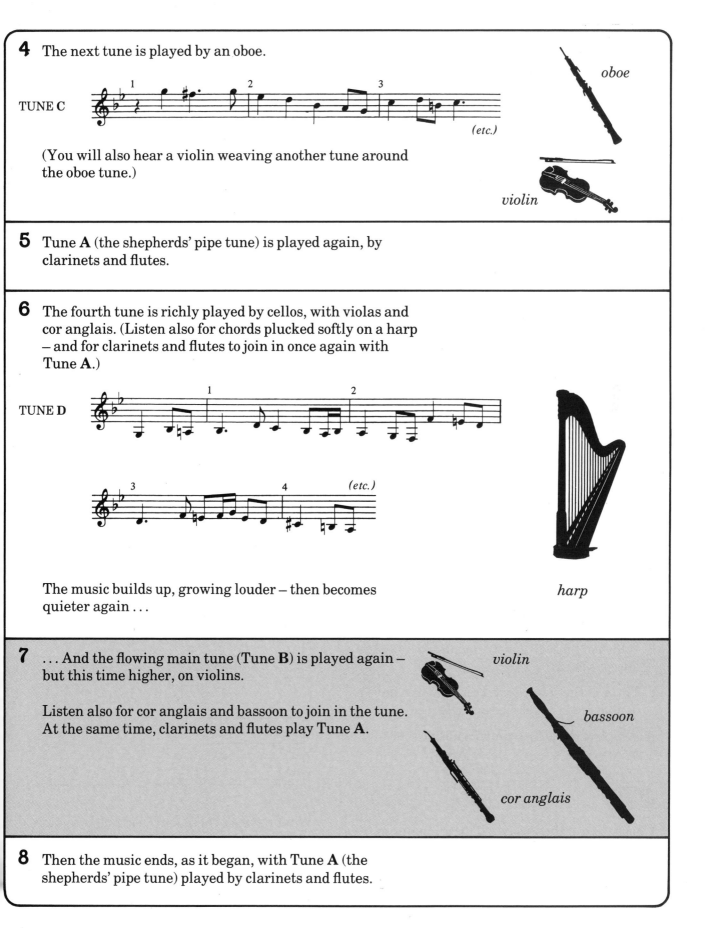

oboe

(You will also hear a violin weaving another tune around the oboe tune.)

violin

5 Tune **A** (the shepherds' pipe tune) is played again, by clarinets and flutes.

6 The fourth tune is richly played by cellos, with violas and cor anglais. (Listen also for chords plucked softly on a harp – and for clarinets and flutes to join in once again with Tune **A**.)

TUNE D

harp

The music builds up, growing louder – then becomes quieter again . . .

7 . . . And the flowing main tune (Tune **B**) is played again – but this time higher, on violins.

violin

Listen also for cor anglais and bassoon to join in the tune. At the same time, clarinets and flutes play Tune **A**.

bassoon

cor anglais

8 Then the music ends, as it began, with Tune **A** (the shepherds' pipe tune) played by clarinets and flutes.

Sheep may safely graze

A

Here are five woodwind instruments you heard during Bach's music called *Sheep may safely graze*:

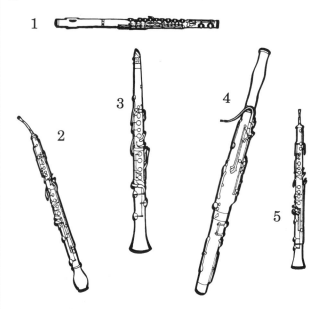

a Match the names to the instruments:

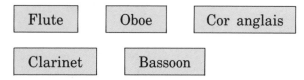

| Flute | Oboe | Cor anglais |

| Clarinet | Bassoon |

b Which of these five instruments can play the lowest sounds?

c Three of these woodwind instruments have a double reed. Which has a *single* reed?

d Which of these instruments has no reed at all?

B

Choose two of the woodwind instruments on this page, and make your own drawings of them. Under each drawing, write the name of the instrument.

C

Listen again to the beginning of Bach's piece called *Sheep may safely graze*. As you listen, answer these questions:

1 The first tune is played by clarinets and flutes. Which family of instruments **accompanies** the tune?

2 The second tune is played by violas, cellos, and cor anglais. Choose two words which match the music:

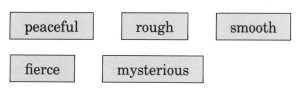

| peaceful | rough | smooth |

| fierce | mysterious |

3 Is this music:
  • fast and quiet?
  • fairly slow and quiet?
  • slow and loud?

D

a Put a letter in each gap to make four more instruments which you hear during *Sheep may safely graze*:

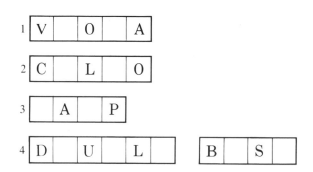

1 | V | | O | | A |

2 | C | | L | | O |

3 | | A | | P | |

4 | D | | U | | L | | B | | S | |

b What have all these four instruments got in common?

c Which of these four instruments is not played with a bow? How is it played?

Grand March

from the opera 'Aida'

Giuseppe VERDI
1813–1901
ITALY

Main characters in the story of 'Aida'

Radamès, captain of the Egyptian Guard
The King of Egypt
Princess Amneris, his daughter
Aida, slave of Princess Amneris
Amonasro, King of Ethiopia

The story of 'Aida' takes place in ancient Egypt, in about 1230 B.C.

The first scene of the opera takes place in the hall of the King's palace at Memphis. The Egyptians have recently defeated the Ethiopians in battle. But the Ethiopians have quickly recovered, and are again attacking Egypt. Radamès, captain of the Egyptian Guard, hopes he will be chosen to lead the army against the Ethiopians. The High Priest tells Radamès that he will consult the goddess Isis to find out who the commander shall be.

The King of Egypt's daughter, Princess Amneris, is in love with Radamès. But Radamès loves Aida – a beautiful Ethiopian girl who was captured in the recent battle, and given to the Princess as a slave.

Princess Amneris comes to speak to Radamès. She is followed by Aida. The Princess guesses that they are in love with each other. She becomes fiercely jealous, and swears vengeance on her slave.

The composer of the opera 'Aida'

Verdi was born in a small village in northern Italy. His father owned the village shop, which also happened to be the local tavern. Verdi was so keen on music that his father bought him an old piano. He soon taught himself to play it.

Verdi never became a good pianist. But he did become very famous as an opera composer. In fact, most people think of him as Italy's greatest opera composer. Three of his best known operas are *Rigoletto*, *Il Trovatore* (The Troubadour), and *Aida*.

Even after Verdi had become world famous, he still enjoyed country life. He bought a farm, and spent as much time there as he could. He loved animals – especially dogs and horses.

The King of Egypt enters, with his priests and courtiers. A messenger rushes in with the news that the Ethiopians are about to attack the sacred city of Thebes. They are led by their king, Amonasro. 'My father!' whispers Aida – but she is not heard by the Egyptians, who do not know that she is a royal princess.

The King announces that the goddess Isis has given her decision. It is that Radamès shall lead the army. Aida is torn between her love for Radamès, and her loyalty to her father and her country.

The Egyptian and Ethiopian armies join in battle. And again the Ethiopians are defeated. The King of Egypt, his court and all the people, go to the gates of the city of Thebes to welcome the victorious Radamès. A Triumphal Arch has been constructed. First to enter through the arch are the Egyptian foot-soldiers. They are followed by the chariots of war. Then come the bearers of the sacred vases, the statues of the gods, and treasures won from the enemy. And finally, Radamès – borne in triumph on a litter carried upon the shoulders of twelve of his captains.

Radamès kneels before the King, who greets him. Then Princess Amneris places the victor's crown upon his head. The Ethiopian prisoners are brought forward. Among them is Amonasro. Aida again exclaims: 'My father!' This time, everyone hears. Amonasro whispers to her that she must not let anyone know he is the king.

8

The King of Egypt says he will grant any wish Radamès cares to make. Radamès would like to ask for Aida's hand in marriage. But instead he asks·that the Ethiopian prisoners should be set free. The King agrees – on condition that Aida and her father are kept as hostages. Then he decrees that Radamès, as reward for his great victory, shall marry Princess Amneris. Radamès and Aida are horrified at this sudden decision. The Princess smiles in triumph at her wretched slave.

It is the night before the wedding of Princess Amneris and Radamès. The Princess, with priests and guards, comes to the Temple of Isis on the banks of the Nile. She will spend the night in prayer.

Aida arrives outside the temple for a last, secret meeting with Radamès. But she has been followed by her father, Amonasro. The Ethiopians are again ready to attack. Amonasro appeals to Aida's loyalty to her own country. He persuades her to get information from Radamès about the movements of the Egyptian army.

Amonasro hides as Radamès arrives. Aida begs Radamès to escape with her to her own country, where they could live in happiness. Radamès eagerly agrees. Aida says they must make sure they avoid the Egyptian army. And Radamès replies that they can leave by way of the Napata pass. It will be deserted until tomorrow – when the Egyptian forces will march through to attack the enemy.

'My men will be there!' mutters Amonasro. And he now steps out of hiding – a shadowy figure in the moonlight. 'Who's there?' demands Radamès. 'Aida's father – and King of the Ethiopians!' replies Amonasro. Radamès realizes with horror that he has betrayed his country. But Princess Amneris has also overheard. She rushes from the temple crying: 'Traitor!' Radamès urges Aida and her father to flee, as the priests and guards arrest him.

The scene changes to the hall of justice in the royal palace. Radamès is brought in, and accused of being a traitor to his country. His judges are the priests. They find him guilty – and condemn him to be buried alive. Princess Amneris desperately pleads for mercy. But it is too late. The priests have more power than the Princess.

Guards take Radamès down into a dark vault, deep below the Temple of Phtha. Above, in the temple itself, Princess Amneris weeps in despair, and prays for Radamès.

The guards leave Radamès in the vault, and begin to seal up the entrance with stones. But Aida has hidden herself in the vault. She is prepared to die with Radamès. He takes her into his arms, as the last heavy stone seals their tomb.

Listen to the *Grand March* from Act 2 of the opera 'Aida'. Here are the words which are sung during the first part:

The people: Glory to Egypt, and to the goddess Isis
who protects our sacred land!
To the King who rules the Delta
songs of joy and praise we sing!
Glory!   Glory!   Glory!
Glory to the King!

Women: Twine the lotus-flower and laurel
to make crowns for the victors' brows!
Let soft showers of fragrant petals
fall upon them as they pass.
Let us dance, Egyptian maidens,
our mysterious circle-dances,
as, around the sun,
the stars dance in the sky!

Priests: Raise your eyes to the gods
who have given our soldiers victory.
Give thanks to the gods this happy day.

Grand March from the opera 'Aida'

An avenue to the city of Thebes. Palm trees, a temple, and a Triumphal Arch. Crowds cheer as the King arrives in state with his courtiers, priests, and slaves carrying huge feather-fans. Princess Amneris arrives, attended by Aida.

1 An exciting fanfare on brass instruments. Then a jerky, rhythmic tune is played by strings and woodwinds:

trumpet

horn

TUNE **A**

Gradually, the music builds up ...

piccolo

2 ... And a triumphant song of praise is sung by all the people:

TUNE **B**

(percussion)

cymbals

bass drum

3 Tune **A** is heard again, as the people loudly sing:
'Glory! ... Glory to the King! ...'

4 A gentler, more flowing tune is sung by the women only:

TUNE C

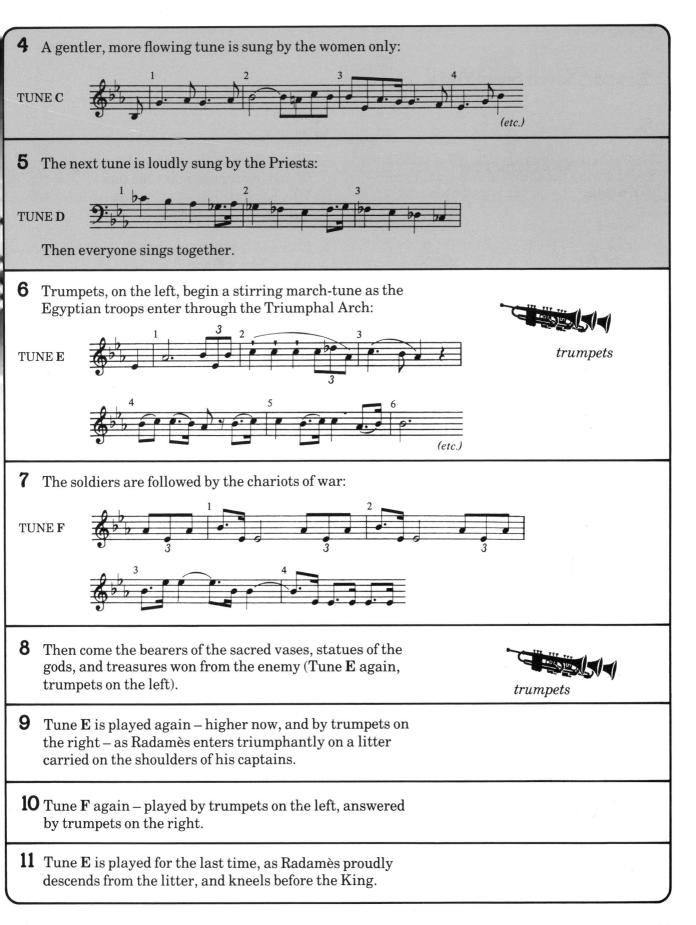

5 The next tune is loudly sung by the Priests:

TUNE D

Then everyone sings together.

6 Trumpets, on the left, begin a stirring march-tune as the Egyptian troops enter through the Triumphal Arch:

TUNE E

trumpets

7 The soldiers are followed by the chariots of war:

TUNE F

8 Then come the bearers of the sacred vases, statues of the gods, and treasures won from the enemy (Tune **E** again, trumpets on the left).

trumpets

9 Tune **E** is played again – higher now, and by trumpets on the right – as Radamès enters triumphantly on a litter carried on the shoulders of his captains.

10 Tune **F** again – played by trumpets on the left, answered by trumpets on the right.

11 Tune **E** is played for the last time, as Radamès proudly descends from the litter, and kneels before the King.

11

Grand March from 'Aida'

A

Name these six instruments. All of them are heard during the *Grand March* from Verdi's opera 'Aida'.

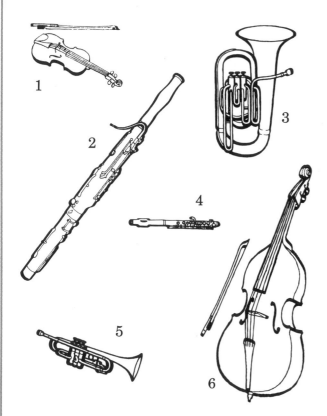

B

The six instruments come from three sections of the orchestra – a pair of instruments from each section.

1 Which two of the instruments are string instruments?
2 Which two are brass instruments?
3 And which two are woodwind instruments?
4 In each of your pairs of instruments:
   - which instrument plays the highest sounds?
   - which one plays the lowest sounds?

C

1 Listen again to the ending of the March. Which instruments play the tunes? Why do you think Verdi chooses these particular instruments?

2 Listen to the music again. You hear two tunes (Tunes E and F on page 11).

   Divide into two groups.
   Group 1: clap the **beat**, steadily, in time to the music.
   Group 2: with your teacher, clap the **rhythm** of the tunes.

3 Listen again – but this time, swap over:
   Group 2 claps the beat;
   Group 1 claps the rhythm.

4 Which did you find easiest – clapping the beat, or clapping the rhythm? Which did you find most enjoyable?

D

Look at this list:

Strings:	O. BELDABUSS
	A. LIVO
Woodwind:	C. I. C. POOL
	N. I. CARTEL
Brass:	M. PUTTER
	B. E. MORTON
Percussion:	D. MURKETTLE
	K. CLOBWOOD

You may think these are eight musicians. But they're not. They're the names of the instruments which they play. The letters in each name have got mixed up. Which instruments are they?

The Hut on Fowl's Legs

from 'Pictures at an Exhibition'

Modest Petrovich
MUSORGSKY
1839–1881
RUSSIA

In 1873, Musorgsky went to a picture exhibition. There were 400 paintings and drawings by an artist friend of his, called Victor Hartmann. Musorgsky was very impressed by the exhibition. A few months later, he composed a set of piano pieces. Each of these pieces vividly describes one of the pictures at the exhibition – the ten pictures which Musorgsky liked the best.

One of the pictures was called 'The Hut on Fowl's Legs'. This was a drawing of a clock. But it was a very special clock. It was designed to look like a hut. On the roof were two cockerels' heads, and the whole thing stood on fowl's legs.

It was, in fact, the hut belonging to the most famous of all Russian witches – Baba Yaga. She lived in a dark forest, and often went off in search of human prey. When she had caught her victims, she would grind up their bones for food!

The composer of *The Hut on Fowl's Legs*

Musorgsky was the son of a rich Russian landowner. When he left school, he was sent to a military academy. But he had been taught to play the piano by his mother, and he went on having piano lessons at the academy.

When Musorgsky was 17, he left the military academy and joined the Regiment of Guards. By now he was a brilliant pianist, and had also begun to compose. He made friends with many Russian musicians, including Borodin and Rimsky-Korsakov.

When he was 19, Musorgsky decided to give up his career as a soldier, and to become a full-time composer.

Listen to Musorgsky's piece called *The Hut on Fowl's Legs*. Musorgsky makes his music sound as if Baba Yaga, by her magic, makes her hut move, and run along on its fowl's legs – and then fly swiftly through the air as she seeks out her prey . . .

Musorgsky wrote this piece to be played on a piano. But you will hear it in a vividly colourful version for orchestra, by the French composer Maurice Ravel. Follow the chart on the next two pages as you listen to the music.

The Hut on Fowl's Legs

1 At Baba Yaga's magic command, the hut on fowl's legs
begins to move with a pounding, hopping rhythm:

kettle drum

TUNE **A**

TUNE **B**

The hut rises, and takes flight.

bass drum

2 A triumphant fanfare, screamed out by three trumpets,
as Baba Yaga spots her prey:

TUNE **C**

trumpets

3 There are menacing calls on horns and trombones
as Baba Yaga pursues her victim.

horn   *trombone*

4 The hut swoops down, and comes to rest
in a lonely forest glade.

snare drum

cymbal   *triangle*

5 The hopping rhythm of Tune **A** is heard again, but the music is quieter now – as Baba Yaga stealthily stalks her victim:

TUNE **D**

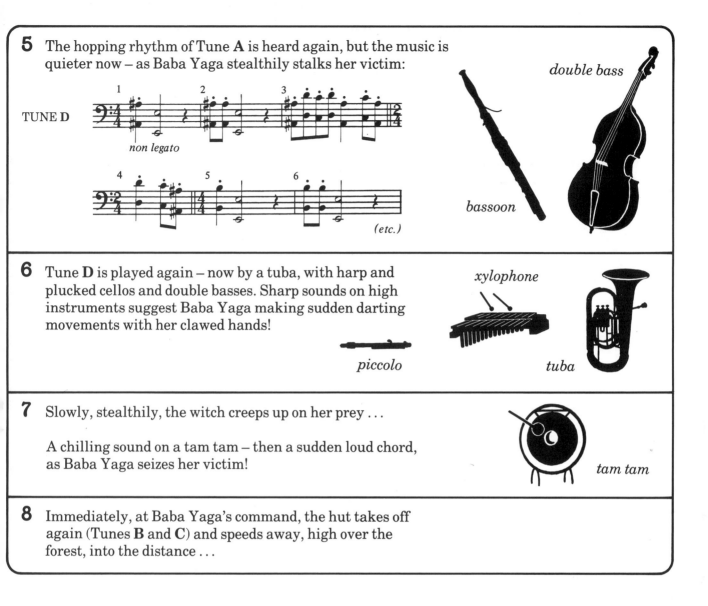

non legato

(etc.)

double bass

bassoon

6 Tune **D** is played again – now by a tuba, with harp and plucked cellos and double basses. Sharp sounds on high instruments suggest Baba Yaga making sudden darting movements with her clawed hands!

xylophone

piccolo

tuba

7 Slowly, stealthily, the witch creeps up on her prey . . .

A chilling sound on a tam tam – then a sudden loud chord, as Baba Yaga seizes her victim!

tam tam

8 Immediately, at Baba Yaga's command, the hut takes off again (Tunes **B** and **C**) and speeds away, high over the forest, into the distance . . .

The Hut on Fowl's Legs

A

During Musorgsky's piece *The Hut on Fowl's Legs* you hear these percussion instruments. (These are instruments which are struck or shaken, crashed or banged.) Name each instrument:

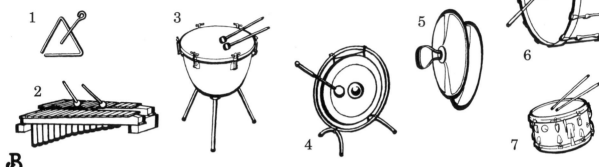

B

When any instrument is played, something is being made to **vibrate**. The vibrations make the sound.
When percussion instruments are played, it is **skin**, or **metal**, or **wood**, which is vibrating to make the sound.

Draw three columns in your notebook, and write these three headings at the top:

Skin	Metal	Wood

Now take each instrument drawn on this page and write its name in the correct column on your chart. (You may find an instrument needs to be written in more than *one* column.)

C

Draw and colour a picture of Baba Yaga's cottage – The Hut on Fowl's Legs.

D

Listen to another of Musorgsky's 'Pictures at an Exhibition', called *The Market Place at Limoges*. You will hear all the hustle and bustle of a colourful, crowded French market, with people busily buying and selling, and housewives gossiping and quarrelling – and even coming to blows! (Listen out for some colourful-sounding percussion instruments in this music.)

Hungarian Dance No.6

Johannes BRAHMS
1833–1897
GERMANY

By the time Brahms was 17, he was playing the piano at concerts. Sometimes he performed on his own, and sometimes he played piano accompaniments for other musicians. He met a Hungarian violinist called Reményi, who was half gypsy and had a fiery temper. Brahms and Reményi decided to go on tour, travelling from city to city and giving concerts of music for violin and piano.

During his travels, Brahms became very interested in Hungarian music. He jotted down many of the tunes he heard. Later, he composed a set of *Hungarian Dances*. In these pieces, Brahms used the gypsy tunes he had heard, and also the rhythms of various Hungarian dances.

The composer of *Hungarian Dance No.6*

Brahms was born in Hamburg. He was the son of a double bass player. His father wanted him to become a musician, too. And so Brahms learned to play the violin, cello, horn, and piano.

Before he was 14, Brahms was earning money by playing the piano in taverns in the dock area of Hamburg. He also spent as much time as possible composing music. His piano teacher said he could become a famous pianist – 'if only he would stop that composing!'

But Brahms was far more interested in writing music than playing the piano. He was to become one of Germany's greatest composers.

Listen to Brahms's *Hungarian Dance No. 6*. Brahms wrote this music for piano duet – two people playing at one piano. But you will hear it in a version for orchestra.

This *Hungarian Dance* is made up of four very different tunes. During the dance, there are many sudden changes of speed, and mood. Sometimes the music is quite slow and soft. Then it will suddenly burst out, very fast and wild. Follow the chart on the next page as you listen to the music.

Hungarian Dance No.6

1 Two loud chords – then the music hesitates, and
the first tune begins quite slowly:

TUNE A

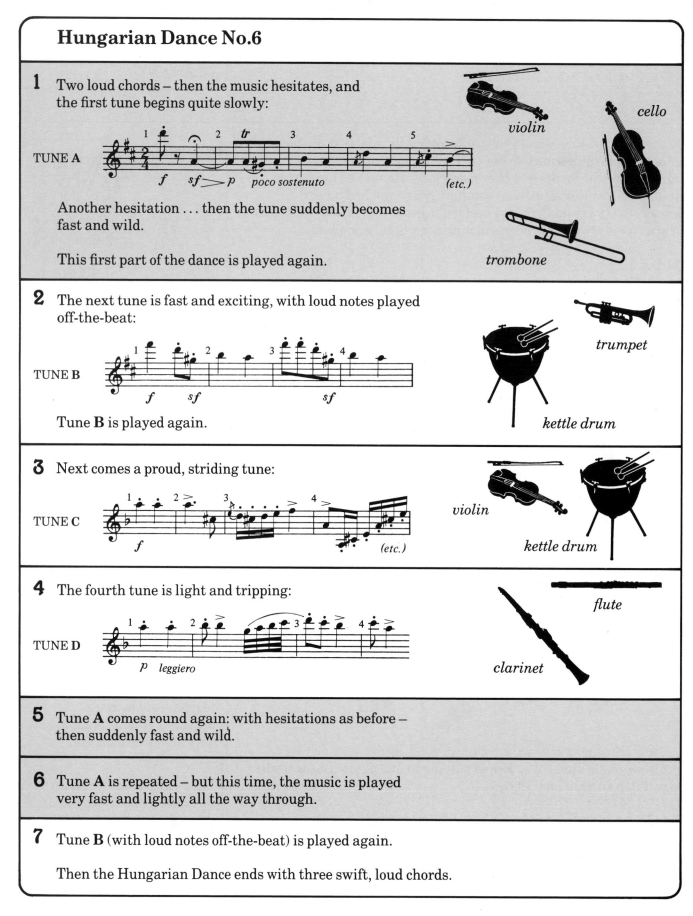

Another hesitation . . . then the tune suddenly becomes
fast and wild.

This first part of the dance is played again.

violin

cello

trombone

2 The next tune is fast and exciting, with loud notes played
off-the-beat:

TUNE B

Tune **B** is played again.

trumpet

kettle drum

3 Next comes a proud, striding tune:

TUNE C

violin

kettle drum

4 The fourth tune is light and tripping:

TUNE D

flute

clarinet

5 Tune **A** comes round again: with hesitations as before –
then suddenly fast and wild.

6 Tune **A** is repeated – but this time, the music is played
very fast and lightly all the way through.

7 Tune **B** (with loud notes off-the-beat) is played again.

Then the Hungarian Dance ends with three swift, loud chords.

18

Hungarian Dance No.6

A

Here are three instruments you heard during Brahms's *Hungarian Dance No. 6*.

1

2

3

f—u—e

—r—m—e—

c—l—o

a string instrument

a woodwind instrument

a brass instrument

1 Put a letter for each dash to make the name of each instrument.
2 Match each instrument to one of the boxes.

B

Among the letters around the circle, find the name of the instrument drawn in the centre. (This is the only percussion instrument you hear during Brahms's *Hungarian Dance No. 6*.)

Can you also find three words which are important to the way this instrument makes its sound?

(Some letters will have to be used more than once.)

C

Listen again to the beginning of *Hungarian Dance No. 6*.

1 The first tune is played twice. Do you find that:
   - the music is always fast?
   - the music is always quite slow?
   - the music often changes speed?

2 How is the second tune different from the first tune?

3 Listen again. And beat time to the music, two beats to a bar, with your right hand. (Use both hands if you like.)

   Listen very carefully, and keep in time with the orchestra. After the second beat, the music hesitates . . . and then moves quite slowly. Later, be ready for the fast bit!

The Pirates of Penzance

Sir Arthur SULLIVAN
1842–1900
ENGLAND

Main characters in the story of 'The Pirates of Penzance'

Frederick, a young Pirate
The Pirate King
Ruth, the Pirates' maid-of-all-work
Major-General Stanley
Mabel, one of his daughters
The Sergeant of the Penzance Police

The story

The first scene takes place on a rocky beach on the coast of
Cornwall. The Pirates are drinking wine to celebrate Frederick's
21st birthday. Today he completes his apprenticeship to them, and
at last becomes a true Pirate.

The Pirate King claps Frederick on the back, and congratulates
him. But Frederick is not happy. He says he has decided to leave the
pirate band. It was a mistake to join them in the first place. Ruth,
who was his nurse when he was a child, agrees. She says his parents
instructed her to apprentice him to a *pilot*. But being a bit deaf, she
thought they said a *pirate*. When she realized her mistake, she was
afraid of being punished. And so she, too, stayed with the Pirates,
and became their maid-of-all-work.

Sir Arthur Sullivan

Sullivan was the son of an
army bandmaster. He went
to music college, and then
became an organist,
conductor and composer.
But Sullivan did not achieve
true fame until he met the
writer, W. S. Gilbert.

They decided to write a
comic opera. Gilbert wrote
the words, and Sullivan set
them to music. This was a
great success. And over the
next 22 years they wrote
another 13 comic operas.
Three of the most famous
are called *The Mikado,
The Gondoliers*, and
The Pirates of Penzance.

W. S. Gilbert

Frederick explains to the Pirates that he has great affection for them all. But he cannot agree with their way of life. In any case, they don't seem to be able to make piracy pay. All the pirates are orphans – and they spare all *other* orphans. This is very well known for miles around. So whenever the Pirates board a ship, all the sailors say that *they* are orphans too!

The Pirates leave. And a group of lovely girls comes onto the beach. Among them are the four daughters of Major-General Stanley. Their names are Mabel, Kate, Edith and Isabel. The girls are preparing to paddle, when they notice Frederick. They are very much attracted by his good looks – and Mabel immediately falls in love with him.

Suddenly the Pirates return. They seize the girls, saying that they will marry them straight away. But Mabel tells them that her father is a Major-General. So the Pirates had better beware!

Major-General Stanley arrives. He is horrified when he hears that the Pirates intend to marry the girls. But he knows the Pirates' weakness. He tells them that he, too, is an orphan. This, of course, is a monstrous and cowardly lie. But the Pirates believe him. They are overcome with pity, and let the Major-General and the girls go free.

The scene changes to a ruined chapel on Major-General Stanley's estate. It is moonlight. The Major-General is bitterly ashamed of the lie he told. He humbly kneels before the tombs of his ancestors – except that they are not really *his* ancestors. He took them over when he bought the estate, several years ago. He is joined by his daughters and Frederick.

Frederick announces that he is about to lead an expedition against the Pirates. The party will be made up of members of the Penzance Police, and their gallant Sergeant.

At this moment, the Police arrive. But they don't seem to be too keen on the task which lies ahead of them. After being given some encouragement, they go off. Frederick is about to follow, when the Pirate King and Ruth suddenly appear. Frederick is alarmed to see that they are pointing pistols at him!

The Pirate King informs Frederick that a very strange fact has come to light. Frederick was born in a leap year – on the 29th of February. This means that he has only had five true birthdays, and so is only 5¼ years old! Therefore he is still apprenticed to the Pirates.

Frederick is horrified. But his strong sense of duty tells him that he must rejoin the pirate band. He also feels he must tell the Pirate King about the Major-General's lie. The Pirate King is furious. He leaves with Ruth to prepare an attack on the Major-General's castle.

Mabel returns. Frederick tells her what has happened. He swears his love for her. And promises to return and marry her when, according to leap-year reckoning, he reaches his 21st birthday. (This would be in 63 years time!) Frederick goes off to rejoin the Pirates.

The Police come back. Mabel now decides to do *her* duty, and informs them that Frederick has rejoined the pirate band. At first, the Police are none too pleased. But then they sympathize. Being policemen, *they* understand all about duty! They will press on – with or without Frederick.

At this moment, the Pirates, including Frederick, are heard approaching 'with cat-like tread'. The Police quickly hide. Then Major-General Stanley and the girls return, all in their night-clothes. The Pirates pounce on the Major-General, and threaten him with death.

The Police now jump out – but are swiftly overpowered by the pirates. In desperation, the Sergeant charges the Pirates to give themselves up 'in the Queen's name'. And, astonishingly, they do so!

Then Ruth rushes in, and reveals another secret. The Pirates are not orphans after all. They are noblemen, who have gone wrong. But being noblemen, they are all, of course, most suitable to marry the girls. Major-General Stanley gladly agrees. And all ends very happily.

Listen to a song with chorus from 'The Pirates of Penzance'. The Penzance Police are making ready to march against the Pirates. The Sergeant addresses his men. With their hands clasped behind their backs – and with a great deal of knees-bending – they echo the last bit of each line of the song, and join in the chorus.

A Policeman's Lot Is Not a Happy One

When a felon's not engaged in his employment *(his employment)*,
Or maturing his felonious little plans *(little plans)*,
His capacity for innocent enjoyment *(-cent enjoyment)*,
Is just as great as any honest man's *(honest man's)*.

Our feelings we with difficulty smother *(-culty smother)*,
When constabulary duty's to be done *(to be done)*.
Ah, take one consideration with another *(with another!)*
A policeman's lot is not a happy one.

Ah! ... When constabulary duty's to be done, to be done,
A policeman's lot is not a happy one, happy one!

When the enterprising burglar's not a-burgling *(not a-burgling)*,
When the cut-throat isn't occupied in crime *(-pied in crime)*,
He loves to hear the little brook a-gurgling *(brook a-gurgling)*,
And listen to the merry village chime *(village chime)*.

When the coster's finished jumping on his mother *(on his mother)*,
He loves to lie a-basking in the sun *(in the sun)*.
Ah, take one consideration with another *(with another!)*
A policeman's lot is not an 'appy one.

Ah! ... When constabulary duty's to be done, to be done,
A policeman's lot is not a happy one, happy one!

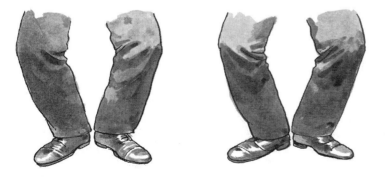

Here is another chorus from *The Pirates of Penzance*. The Police
quickly hide – as the Pirates approach 'with cat-like tread'. But they
sing rather loudly! (And another part of the fun is that, every now
and then, the orchestra plays a loud, crashing chord.)

With Cat-like Tread

Pirates: With cat-like tread upon our prey we steal;
In silence dread our cautious way we feel!
No sound at all, we never speak a word;
A fly's footfall would be distinctly heard!

Police: Tarantara, tarantara!

Pirates: So stealthily the Pirate creeps,
While all the household soundly sleeps.

[As the Pirates sing the Chorus, the Police sing 'Ra, ra, ra, ra ...']

CHORUS

A Pirate:	Here's your crow-bar, and your centre-bit,
	Your life preserver, you may want to hit!
	Your silent matches, your dark lantern seize!
	Take your file and your skeletonic keys!

Police:	Tarantara . . .
Pirates:	With cat-like tread . . .
Police:	Tarantara!
Pirates:	In silence dread . . .

Pirates:	With cat-like tread upon our prey we steal;
	In silence dread our cautious way we feel!
	No sound at all, we never speak a word;
	A fly's footfall would be distinctly heard!

[Then the Police sing 'Tarantara, ra, ra . . .' as the Pirates sing the Chorus:]

Chorus:	Come, friends, who plough the sea,
	Truce to navigation, take another station;
	Let's vary piracee with a little burglaree!
	With cat-like tread
	Upon our prey we steal;
	In silence dread
	Our cautious way we feel!

Music from The Pirates of Penzance

A

1 Listen again to 'A Policeman's Lot Is Not a Happy One'. Join in with the Police as they echo the last bit of each line and sing the chorus.

2 Try it again – this time, for more fun, standing up with your hands clasped behind your back. Do a knees-bend on each strong beat you sing!

B

Crossword

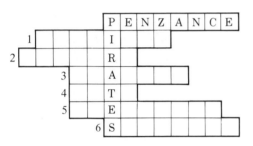

Use these clues to fill in the missing words:

1 He composed the music of the operetta *The Pirates of Penzance*.
2 This man wrote the words of the songs.
3 The name of Mabel's father is Major-General . . . .
4 The Pirates' maid-of-all-work is called . . . .
5 He was made an apprentice Pirate.
6 The Police are led by a . . . .

C

Listen again to 'With Cat-like Tread'.

During the first part: clap the beat, very softly – **except** when the orchestra plays a crashing chord. Every time this happens, make a very loud clap!

When the chorus comes: clap the beat, loudly – and also whistle the tune.

D

Listen to a song from another comic opera by Gilbert and Sullivan, called *Ruddigore*. (The words are printed opposite.)

The time is midnight, and the scene is the ghostly, dimly-lit portrait gallery of Ruddigore Castle. The walls are covered with large portraits of all the previous Baronets of Ruddigore, including the one who died most recently, Sir Roderic. The portraits come to life – and step down from their frames! Led by Sir Roderic, they join in this rather gruesome song.

(Read through the words, with your teacher, before listening to the song.)

E

Which instruments are these?

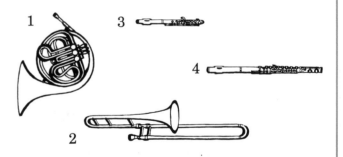

Listen again to 'When the Night Wind Howls', and you will hear that Sullivan uses these instruments in a rather special and vivid way – to bring out the meaning of certain words which are being sung.

F

Imagine that new records of *The Pirates of Penzance*, and *Ruddigore*, by Gilbert and Sullivan, will soon be on sale in the shops. Draw and colour a picture which could be used on the cover of one of these records.

'When the Night Wind Howls'

from the comic opera *Ruddigore*

Sir Roderic: When the night wind howls in the chimney cowls,
And the bat in the moonlight flies,
And inky clouds, like funeral shrouds,
Sail over the midnight skies—
When the footpads quail at the night-bird's wail,
And black dogs bay at the moon,
Then is the spectre's holiday—
Then is the ghost's high noon!

Chorus: *Ha! ha!*

Sir Roderic: For then is the ghost's high noon!

Chorus: *Ha! ha!   High noon . . .*
Then is the ghosts' high noon!

Sir Roderic: As the sob of the breeze sweeps over the trees
And the mists lie low on the fen,
From grey tomb-stones are gathered the bones
That once were women and men.
And away they go, with a mop and a mow,
To the revel that ends too soon,
For cock-crow limits our holiday—
The dead of the night's high noon!

Chorus: *Ha! ha!*

Sir Roderic: The dead of the night's high noon!

Chorus: *Ha! ha!   High noon . . .*
The dead of the night's high noon!

Sir Roderic: And then each ghost with his ladye-toast
To their churchyard beds take flight,
With a kiss, perhaps, on her lantern chaps,
And a grisly grim "good night!"
Till the welcome knell of the midnight bell
Rings forth its jolliest tune,
And ushers in our next high holiday—
The dead of the night's high noon!

Chorus: *Ha! ha!*

Sir Roderic: The dead of the night's high noon!

Chorus: *Ha! ha!   High noon . . .*
The dead of the night's high noon!
Ha! ha!   Ha! ha!

Aubade

from the opera 'Le Cid'

Jules MASSENET
1842–1912
FRANCE

Most countries have a national hero – perhaps more than one. The national hero of Switzerland is William Tell. For England, you might think of Robin Hood, and King Arthur.

The national hero of Spain is Rodrigo Díaz de Bivar. He lived during the 11th century, and became famous for his exploits in battle – especially against the Moors, who were invading Spain. People called him *El Cid*, which means 'conqueror'. He was very brave, but also boastful, and cruel. In those days, each region of Spain had its own king. Sometimes the Cid fought for one king, sometimes for another. He said all kings were the same to him – provided they rewarded him well for his services.

On one occasion, the Cid fought for the King of Saragossa and captured the city of Valencia for him. Later, the Cid was banished from the city. So he recaptured it, after a long and cruel siege – and then ruled there as king himself, with his army of 7,000 chosen soldiers.

Many stories were told about the Cid. Some were true, and some were legends. One tells of his favourite sword, which he called *Tizona*, meaning 'terror of the world'. Another tells of his horse, called *Babieca*. It lived for two-and-a-half years after the Cid had died – but no one else was ever allowed to ride it.

The composer of the opera 'Le Cid'

Massenet was taught to play the piano by his mother. When he was 11, he became a student at the famous music college called the Paris Conservatoire.

What Massenet wanted most was to become a composer. But when he left the music college, he found it difficult to earn much money. So he also played the piano in cafés. And sometimes he was hired as an extra percussion player at the Paris Opéra.

Massenet wrote many songs, and pieces for orchestra. But he was most interested in composing operas. He wrote more than 30 of them, and became one of France's most famous opera composers.

The Cid died in 1099. Eight centuries later, the French composer Massenet wrote an opera about him, entitled 'Le Cid'. One scene of the opera takes place in the square of a town in northern Spain. It is a sunny spring morning, and a festival is taking place. Townsfolk and peasants perform dances from different parts of Spain. Listen to one of these Spanish dances. It is called *Aubade*, which means 'dawn music'.

Aubade from 'Le Cid'

1 First, a crisp introduction – listen for piccolo and triangle.

piccolo

triangle

2 The first tune is played mainly by clarinets, with a bouncing accompaniment for the strings of the orchestra.

(All through this piece, the string instruments are plucked – suggesting the strumming of a Spanish guitar.)

violin

clarinet

double bass

TUNE A

3 The high, clear sounds of piccolo and triangle are heard again in the second tune:

piccolo

triangle

TUNE B

4 The next tune begins with plucked chords – sounding again like the strumming of a guitar:

clarinet

violin

TUNE C

5 The main tune (Tune **A**) comes round again.

6 The beginning of Tune **B** is heard, twice, on flute and piccolo.

7 Quiet notes on plucked strings and kettle drums.

Listen for a snatch of Tune **A**. Then two loud, stamping chords end the dance.

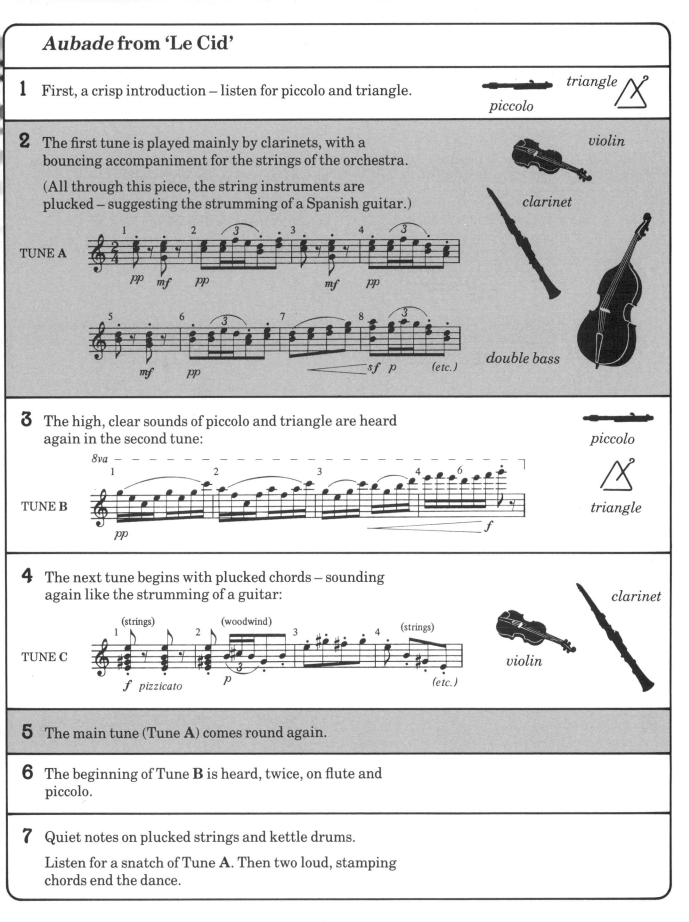

Le Cid

A

Listen to part of another dance from 'Le Cid' by Massenet. The dance is called *Madrilène* – meaning 'a dance from Madrid'.

These are the main tunes you will hear:

If **you** were taking part in this Spanish dance, would you find that:
- the music is fast all the way through?
- the music is always quite slow?
- the speed sometimes changes?

B

1 Listen to the *Madrilène* again. As you listen, write down the names of:
- three instruments playing tunes;
- three instruments which are playing the accompaniment to the tunes.

2 Which instruments does Massenet use in this dance to make the music sound Spanish?

C

Here are the names of the two dances you have heard from Massenet's 'Le Cid':

(1) *Aubade* – dawn music
(2) *Madrilène* – a dance from Madrid

Which dance did you like the best? Why?

D

Here are some of the instruments you heard in the two dances from 'Le Cid':

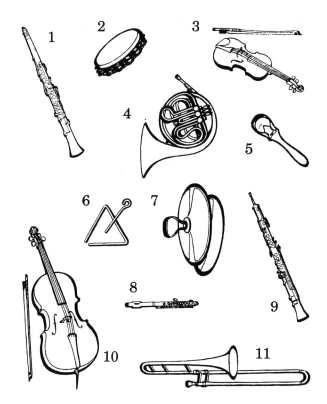

a Name each instrument.
b Which of them are string instruments?
c Which are brass instruments?
d Which are percussion instruments?
e And which are woodwind instruments?
f Draw four of these instruments – choosing one from each section of the orchestra.

March: Semper Fidelis

John Philip SOUSA
1854–1932
USA

Many of Sousa's pieces are marches – he composed 136 of them! Their catchy tunes and bright rhythms are known by millions of people all over the world. It was because of these pieces that Sousa became known as 'The March King'. Here are the names of some of Sousa's most famous marches:

Semper Fidelis ('Always Faithful')
The Liberty Bell
The Washington Post
The Thunderer
The Stars and Stripes Forever

Sousa's marches are for military band. This kind of band is made up of brass, woodwind and percussion instruments – but no string instruments.

Military bands vary in the number, and different kinds, of instruments which are used. For example, a military band might be made up of these instruments:

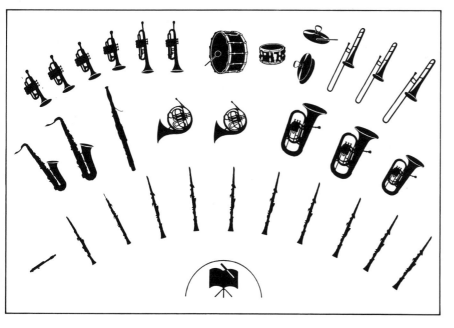

back row: 4 cornets, 2 trumpets, bass drum, snare drum, cymbals, 3 trombones.
middle row: 2 saxophones, bassoon, 2 horns, 2 tubas, euphonium.
front row: piccolo, small clarinet, oboe, 8 clarinets.

(Another military band might include more instruments than these.)

The composer of the March: *Semper Fidelis*

Sousa's father was a trombone player in the US Marine Band in Washington. He taught his son to play several kinds of wind instrument. Sousa also learned to play the violin, and studied music at a music college. He also began to compose.

Later, Sousa became the conductor of a theatre orchestra in Washington. Then at the age of only 26 he was invited to become the conductor of the US Marine Band.

12 years later he formed his own band, called Sousa's Band. He took his band on several tours of America and Europe. Then in 1910 he took it on a long tour, playing in many different countries all over the world.

March: Semper Fidelis

This famous march by Sousa is the official march of the US Marines. Its title, which means 'Always Faithful', is their motto.

1 First, a short introduction – bright and rousing.

piccolo

snare drum

cymbals

2 Then the first tune of the march is played with a brisk, light-stepping rhythm:

TUNE **A**

clarinet

snare drum

cymbals

trumpet

tuba

This first tune is played again.

3 The next tune is shared between high-sounding brass and woodwind instruments:

TUNE **B**

trumpet

piccolo

cornet

clarinet

cymbals

Tune **B** is played again.

4 An exciting **interlude** – crisply played on snare drum and cymbal only.

snare drum   *cymbal*

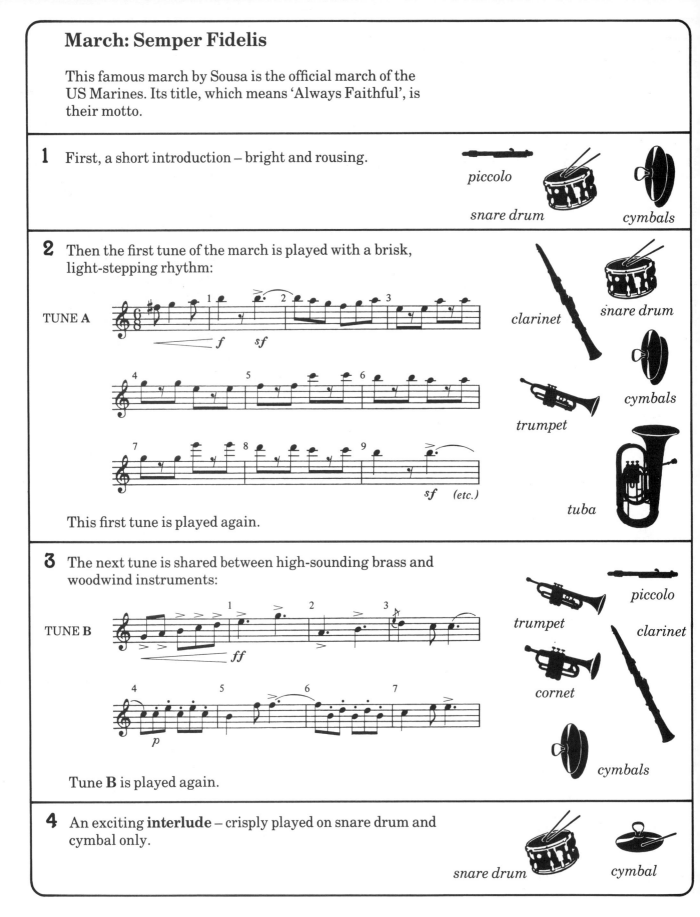

5 Then comes a fanfare-like tune, played by trumpets and cornets. (Listen also for low-sounding instruments, playing over and over again a snatch of tune made up of climbing notes.)

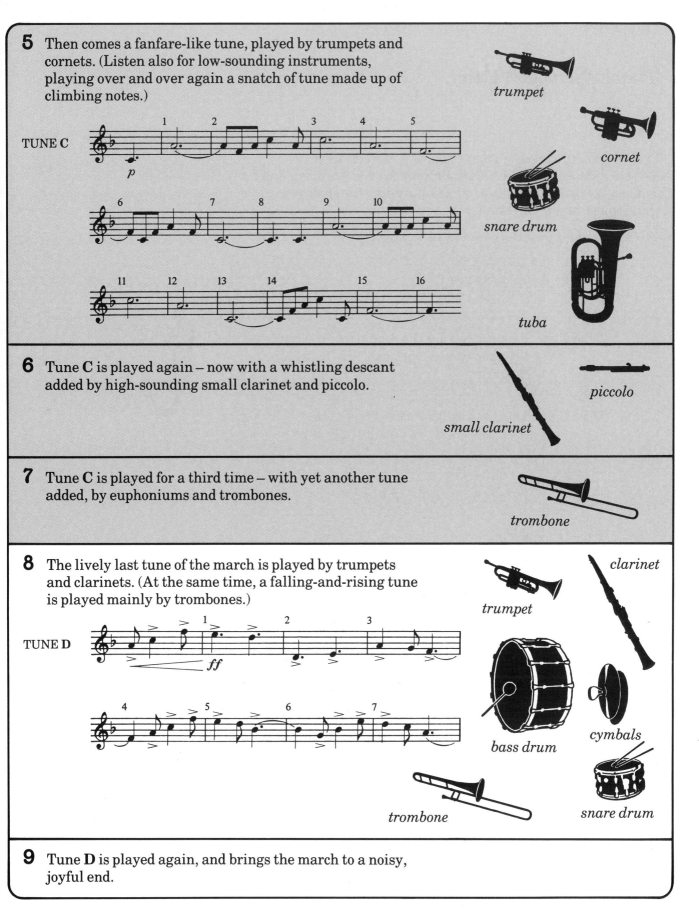

trumpet

cornet

snare drum

tuba

TUNE C

6 Tune **C** is played again – now with a whistling descant added by high-sounding small clarinet and piccolo.

piccolo

small clarinet

7 Tune **C** is played for a third time – with yet another tune added, by euphoniums and trombones.

trombone

8 The lively last tune of the march is played by trumpets and clarinets. (At the same time, a falling-and-rising tune is played mainly by trombones.)

TUNE D

trumpet

clarinet

bass drum

cymbals

snare drum

trombone

9 Tune **D** is played again, and brings the march to a noisy, joyful end.

March: Semper Fidelis

A

Listen again to the second part of Sousa's march called *Semper Fidelis*. After the 'interlude' played on snare drum and cymbal, you will hear Tune C (the fanfare-like tune) played three times, and then Tune D played twice.

Do these actions as these two tunes are played:

1	Tune **C**	Clap the beat: | **One two** | **One two** | **One two** | (and so on)
2	Tune **C**	Imagine you are the conductor, and conduct the band by beating time – two beats to each bar:
3	Tune **C**	This time, sing or whistle the tune. (Perhaps some of you could play it on recorders.)
4	Tune **D**	Conduct the band – two beats to each bar.
5	Tune **D**	Clap the beat – One two, One two (and so on).

B

The brass instrument drawn on the right, called a **sousaphone**, was invented by Sousa himself. When the sousaphone is included in a band, it plays deep-sounding notes, like the bass tuba. To play the sousaphone, as you can see, you have to put your right arm and head through the middle of the instrument – so that it looks as if it has wound itself right round you!

Invent a musical instrument of your own.

How will your instrument make its sounds?
Will it be struck? Or played with a bow?
Or will it, like Sousa's instrument, be blown?

What will you call **your** instrument?

sousaphone

Things to do

C

1 Name four (or more) wind instruments which you are likely to hear playing in a military band.
2 Name two (or more) percussion instruments which are likely to join in.
3 What is the main difference between the sound of a military band and the sound of an orchestra?

D

Listen to an arrangement of another famous march by Sousa, called *The Stars and Stripes Forever*. This march is extremely popular in the USA. Americans think of it as their second national anthem (in the same way as the British think of 'Land of Hope and Glory' as Britain's second national anthem.)

During Sousa's March *The Stars and Stripes Forever* you will hear these four tunes:

You will hear these four tunes played in this order:

A	A	B	B	C	D	C	D	C

E Crossword

Fill in all the missing letters to make the names of six instruments. Each of them takes part in the recording of Sousa's March *The Stars and Stripes Forever*.

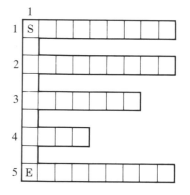

These drawings are the clues to the crossword:

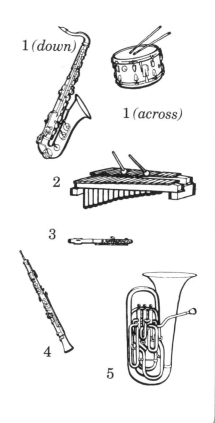

1 (down)

1 (across)

2

3

4

5

Conversation between Beauty and the Beast

from the suite 'Mother Goose'

Maurice RAVEL
1875–1937
FRANCE

Ravel's music called 'Mother Goose' is made up of five different pieces. Here are their titles:

(1) Sleeping Beauty's Pavan.
(2) Tom Thumb
(3) Little Ugly, Empress of the Pagodas
(4) Conversation between Beauty and the Beast
(5) The Magic Garden (the Prince awakens Sleeping Beauty)

The five pieces illustrate scenes from French fairy-tales, written more than 250 years ago. (You may recognize one or two of them as the stories of Christmas pantomimes.)

Ravel first wrote 'Mother Goose' for piano duet – two people playing at one piano. When the pieces were first performed at a concert, they were played by two very young pianists, aged six and ten. Later, Ravel made a version of the music to be played by a full orchestra.

Listen to the fourth piece, the one about Beauty and the Beast, in the version for orchestra. The fairy-tale tells how Beauty's love for the ugly, but kind-hearted Beast breaks a magic spell, and transforms him into a handsome prince.

The composer of the suite 'Mother Goose'

Ravel was born in a small village in southern France, near the Spanish border. When he was 12, his family moved to Paris. He began to study music, and later became one of France's most famous composers.

Ravel composed a fairly small number of pieces. He wrote several of them first for piano, and then later made versions of them to be played by an orchestra.

Ravel gives each of the two characters in the story a special tune. You will hear Beauty's tune played first by a clarinet – a woodwind instrument which has a single reed. The Beast's tune is growled out by a double bassoon. This instrument has a double reed, and it plays the deepest notes in the woodwind section of the orchestra. The double bassoon's lengthy tube, which is folded in four, is 5.6 metres long – double the length of the ordinary bassoon.

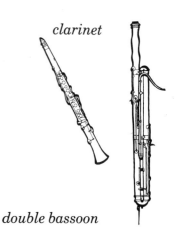

clarinet

double bassoon

Conversation between Beauty and the Beast

1 Beauty's tune (which is quite lengthy) is a swaying waltz-tune, played smoothly by a clarinet:

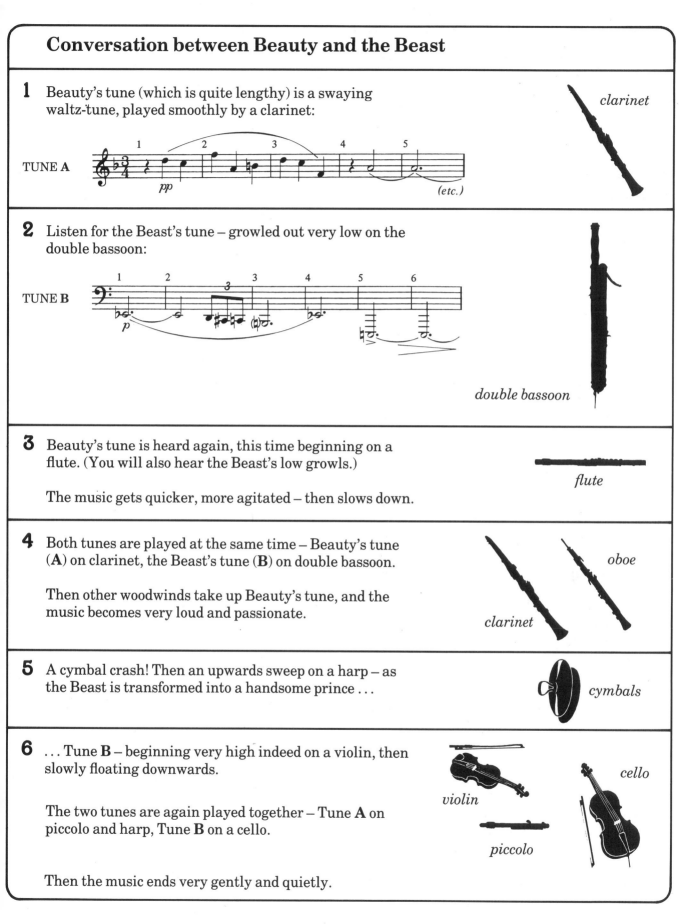 *clarinet*

TUNE A

2 Listen for the Beast's tune – growled out very low on the double bassoon:

TUNE B

double bassoon

3 Beauty's tune is heard again, this time beginning on a flute. (You will also hear the Beast's low growls.)

flute

The music gets quicker, more agitated – then slows down.

4 Both tunes are played at the same time – Beauty's tune (**A**) on clarinet, the Beast's tune (**B**) on double bassoon.

oboe

Then other woodwinds take up Beauty's tune, and the music becomes very loud and passionate.

clarinet

5 A cymbal crash! Then an upwards sweep on a harp – as the Beast is transformed into a handsome prince . . .

cymbals

6 . . . Tune **B** – beginning very high indeed on a violin, then slowly floating downwards.

cello

violin

The two tunes are again played together – Tune **A** on piccolo and harp, Tune **B** on a cello.

piccolo

Then the music ends very gently and quietly.

Conversation between Beauty and the Beast

A

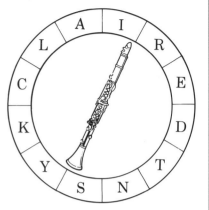

Among the letters around the circle, find the name of the instrument drawn in the centre. (Its sound is often heard during *Conversation between Beauty and the Beast*.)

Can you also find two words which are very important to the way this instrument makes its sound?

(Some letters will have to be used more than once.)

B

In the music called *Conversation between Beauty and the Beast*, each character is given a special tune.

The drawing on the right shows the *shape* of one of these tunes – showing how the notes go higher, or lower, as they make the tune.

1 Listen, as your teacher plays both tunes from this piece of music. Which of the two tunes matches the drawing?

2 Listen again, as your teacher plays the other tune.
   Make your own drawing, to show the shape of this tune.

C

The double bassoon plays the deepest notes in the woodwind section of the orchestra.

1 Which (very tiny) woodwind instrument can play the highest notes?
2 Which instrument plays the deepest notes in the strings section of the orchestra?
3 And which plays the deepest notes in the brass section?

D

double bassoon

Either: draw and colour a picture showing what happens during *Conversation between Beauty and the Beast*.

Or: make your own drawings of the two instruments which play the most important part in the music – the clarinet, and the double bassoon.

Music from the ballet

Petrushka

Igor STRAVINSKY
Born in RUSSIA, 1882
died in USA, 1971

Main characters in the story of 'Petrushka'

The Old Showman
Petrushka
The Ballerina
The Moor

The story of 'Petrushka' takes place in St Petersburg, Russia, in the year 1830.

The story

The first scene of the ballet takes place in a large public square in St Petersburg. It is a sunny afternoon in late winter. The colourful, bustling crowds are enjoying all the fun and excitement of the Shrovetide Fair – the last festival before Lent begins.

There are side-shows of all kinds, and brightly-lit stalls selling sweets and gingerbread, hot pies and cakes. A gypsy is telling fortunes, while a street-dancer spreads out a small carpet and then dances on it, to a tune played on a barrel organ. In the background are swings and slides, and a merry-go-round with shiny, brightly-painted wooden horses.

But the centre of attraction is a little theatre, whose curtains have not yet been opened.

The composer of *Petrushka*

Stravinsky was born in Oranienbaum in Russia. His father wanted him to become a lawyer. And so Stravinsky went to study law in St Petersburg (the city now called Leningrad.)

But he also studied music in his spare time. And he received a great deal of help and advice from the famous Russian composer, Rimsky-Korsakov.

Stravinsky soon became famous as a composer. The Russian ballet producer, Diaghilev, asked him to write music for a ballet based on a Russian fairy tale called *The Firebird*. This was a great success.

During the next two years, Stravinsky wrote another ballet for Diaghilev's company. This is called *Petrushka*. It tells the story of a Russian puppet.

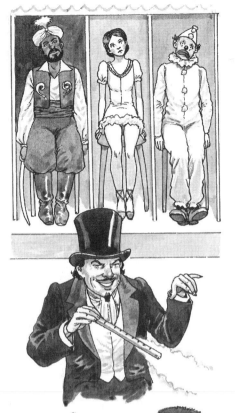

Two drummers, in smart uniforms, beat loudly on their drums. An Old Showman pops his head through the curtains of the little theatre. The crowd becomes silent and watches, as the Showman steps through the curtains. He takes out a flute, and plays a tune. He tells the crowd that it is, in fact, a magic flute. Then he swiftly opens the curtains.

And there, side by side, in separate booths, are three puppets. The first is a Moor, in magnificently colourful costume. The second is a Ballerina with red-painted cheeks and lips. The third is Petrushka – a floppy, ridiculous, sad-faced clown.

The Showman, by his magic, has given his three puppets human feelings and passions. Petrushka is desperately in love with the Ballerina. But the Ballerina prefers the magnificent, but rather stupid, Moor.

The Showman touches each puppet in turn with his magic flute. They twitch into life – and then break into a wild Russian dance. To everyone's amazement, the puppets leave their booths and come down and dance among the crowd. Suddenly, Petrushka is overcome with jealousy. He tries to attack the Moor. But the Showman orders him to stop, and the puppets continue their dancing. Then they return to their booths, and the curtains are swiftly pulled together again.

The second scene takes place in Petrushka's room. The walls are of black cardboard, with silver stars and a moon painted on them. The door flies open, and the Showman brutally kicks Petrushka into a corner. His sawdust body collapses in a heap. The Showman leaves. Slowly and awkwardly, Petrushka picks himself up. With clownish gestures, he tells of his love for the Ballerina. And of his hatred for the Showman, who holds him in his evil power.

Suddenly the Ballerina enters. Petrushka is overcome with joy. He jumps and capers around her. But the Ballerina is frightened by Petrushka's antics, and runs out of the room.

The third scene takes place in the Moor's room. The walls are red, with green palm trees and fantastic fruits painted on them. The Moor, in his splendidly colourful costume, is lying on his back on a couch. He is juggling with a coconut – throwing it up with his feet and catching it with his hands.

The Moor becomes bored. He shakes the coconut and listens. Then he tries to break it open with his scimitar. But he is not successful. He decides that the coconut must contain a very powerful god. He kneels, and prays to it – but falls over.

The door opens and the Ballerina dances in, playing a tune on a toy trumpet. As she waltzes gracefully around the room, the Moor tries to join in. But his dancing is clumsy and ridiculous. He catches the Ballerina and takes her in his arms. The door bursts open again, and Petrushka rushes in. He is mad with jealousy, and feebly threatens the Moor. This throws the Moor into a rage. He grabs his scimitar and chases Petrushka round and round the room, and then out of the door.

The last scene takes place in the square again. Dusk is falling, but there is still much dancing and jollity. A peasant leads in a huge performing bear, which entertains the crowd with its antics. Masked revellers arrive, and prance among the crowd. They wear fantastic costumes – some dressed as devils, others as animals.

Then the crowd falls silent, as frantic noises are heard coming from behind the closed curtains of the little stage. Suddenly Petrushka bursts through the curtains – chased by the enraged Moor, his scimitar raised high. He strikes again and again at poor Petrushka, who collapses to the ground. Everyone gapes, as the body twitches, and trembles, and then becomes still . . .

Someone shrieks: 'Murder!' The Old Showman comes forward. He picks up Petrushka's limp, sawdust body. 'See,' he says, 'it was only a puppet. So how can a murder have been committed?'

The crowd, silent and bewildered, slowly disperses into the gathering darkness. The Showman is left alone, the puppet sagging over his arm. As he turns to go, a mysterious shape appears above the roof of the theatre – white against the dark night sky. It is the ghost of Petrushka, shaking his fists as he curses his cruel master. The Showman stares up in horror. *Was* Petrushka just a puppet after all?

Listen to some colourful music played at the beginning of Scene 4 of 'Petrushka'. The sky is darkening as evening approaches. But the crowds are still eager to enjoy all the fun of the Shrovetide Fair.

In this music, Stravinsky makes use of two old Russian folk-tunes (Tunes A and B, below). Get to know these two tunes before you listen to the music. Sing or play each tune.

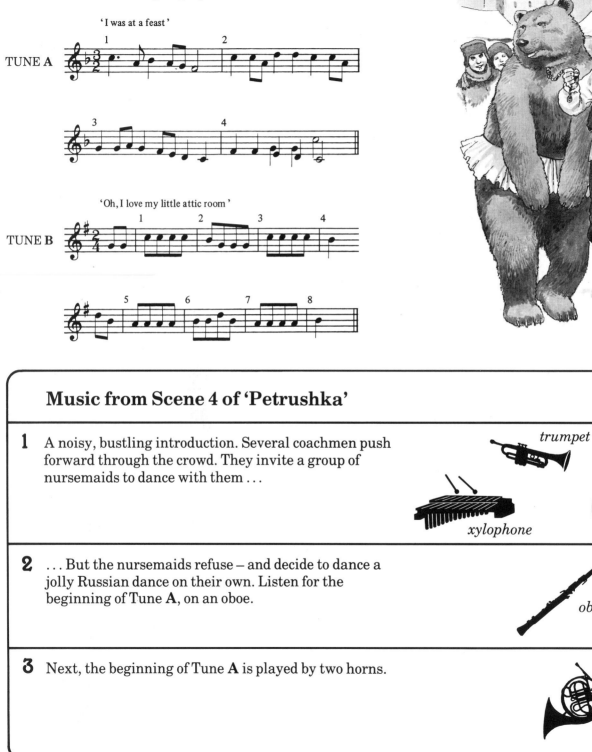

TUNE A 'I was at a feast'

TUNE B 'Oh, I love my little attic room'

Music from Scene 4 of 'Petrushka'

1 A noisy, bustling introduction. Several coachmen push forward through the crowd. They invite a group of nursemaids to dance with them . . .

trumpet

xylophone

horn

2 . . . But the nursemaids refuse – and decide to dance a jolly Russian dance on their own. Listen for the beginning of Tune **A**, on an oboe.

oboe

3 Next, the beginning of Tune **A** is played by two horns.

horn

4 Then (when the double basses join in) Tune **A** is played complete – by violins and horns.

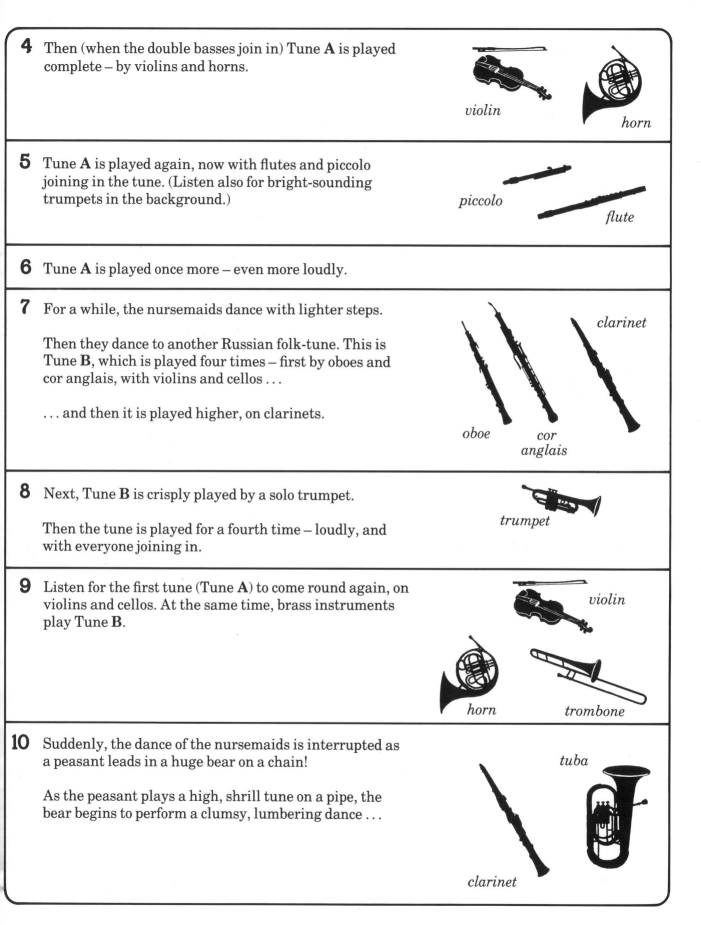

violin

horn

5 Tune **A** is played again, now with flutes and piccolo joining in the tune. (Listen also for bright-sounding trumpets in the background.)

piccolo

flute

6 Tune **A** is played once more – even more loudly.

7 For a while, the nursemaids dance with lighter steps.

Then they dance to another Russian folk-tune. This is Tune **B**, which is played four times – first by oboes and cor anglais, with violins and cellos . . .

. . . and then it is played higher, on clarinets.

clarinet

oboe

cor anglais

8 Next, Tune **B** is crisply played by a solo trumpet.

Then the tune is played for a fourth time – loudly, and with everyone joining in.

trumpet

9 Listen for the first tune (Tune **A**) to come round again, on violins and cellos. At the same time, brass instruments play Tune **B**.

violin

horn

trombone

10 Suddenly, the dance of the nursemaids is interrupted as a peasant leads in a huge bear on a chain!

As the peasant plays a high, shrill tune on a pipe, the bear begins to perform a clumsy, lumbering dance . . .

tuba

clarinet

43

℘etrushka

𝒜

Here are five of the instruments you heard in the music from *Petrushka*.

a Name each instrument.

b Which of these instruments belongs to the strings section of the orchestra?

c Which is a percussion instrument?

d Which **two** instruments belong to the same section of the orchestra? Which section is it?

e Which instrument is a woodwind instrument with a single reed?

ℬ

Design and colour a poster advertising a performance of

> Petrushka
>
> a ballet by Stravinsky

In your poster you could include a drawing of a scene from the ballet. And also, perhaps, some of the instruments which take part in the music.

C

Listen to an exciting dance by another Russian composer, named Glière. It's called *Russian Sailors' Dance*. This music, too, is based on a Russian folk-tune, called 'Little Apple':

After a short introduction, this folk-tune is played over and over again. But each time, you will hear a different combination of instruments. Then there is a very fast and noisy ending to the dance.

1 Listen to the *Russian Sailors' Dance*. Each time you hear the folk-tune, make a tick on a piece of paper, like this:

✓   ✓   ✓   (. . . and so on)

How many times is the folk-tune played?

2 Listen to the music again – and write down the names of any percussion instruments you hear.

March of the Siamese Children

from the musical 'The King and I'

Richard RODGERS
1902–1979
USA

The story of 'The King and I' takes place in 1862, in Siam (the country now known as Thailand). Anna, an English school-teacher, arrives in Bangkok, the capital city of Siam. Anna's husband has recently died, and she has decided to take a new job. She is to become the governess of the King of Siam's children.

Anna is amazed at the splendour of the royal palace. The King greets her, and introduces her to his many wives. Then, in march the royal princes and princesses, one after another – 19 of them altogether. The eldest is called Prince Chulalongkorn.

The composer of *March of the Siamese Children*

Richard Rodgers had his first song published when he was only 14. When he was 17, he went to Columbia University. He became friends with another student called Lorenz Hart.

Instead of working hard to pass their examinations, Rodgers and Hart decided to write musical plays. Hart wrote the words, and Rodgers set them to music. It took them several years to make a success of this. Then they became world famous.

After Hart died, in 1943, Rodgers paired up with another writer, named Oscar Hammerstein II. And this partnership was even more successful.

Among the most famous musicals written by Rodgers and Hammerstein are *Oklahoma!*, *South Pacific*, *The King and I*, and *The Sound of Music*.

At first, Anna finds the King very strange. But as the weeks pass by, they grow to understand one another, and Anna becomes the King's trusted adviser. She makes friends with Lady Thiang, the King's head wife, and also with Tuptim, a beautiful Burmese girl who has been given to the King as a present. But Tuptim loves Lun Tha, a young man from her own country. They meet in secret. When the King finds out, he forbids them to see each other again. This makes Anna so angry, she decides to leave.

However, when the King falls desperately ill, Anna rushes to his side. He dies, and Anna realizes that now she cannot leave. She must stay to help and advise Chulalongkorn – new King of Siam.

March of the Siamese Children

The King of Siam's many children march in to meet Anna for the first time. (The orchestra includes several instruments which make the music sound 'Eastern'.)

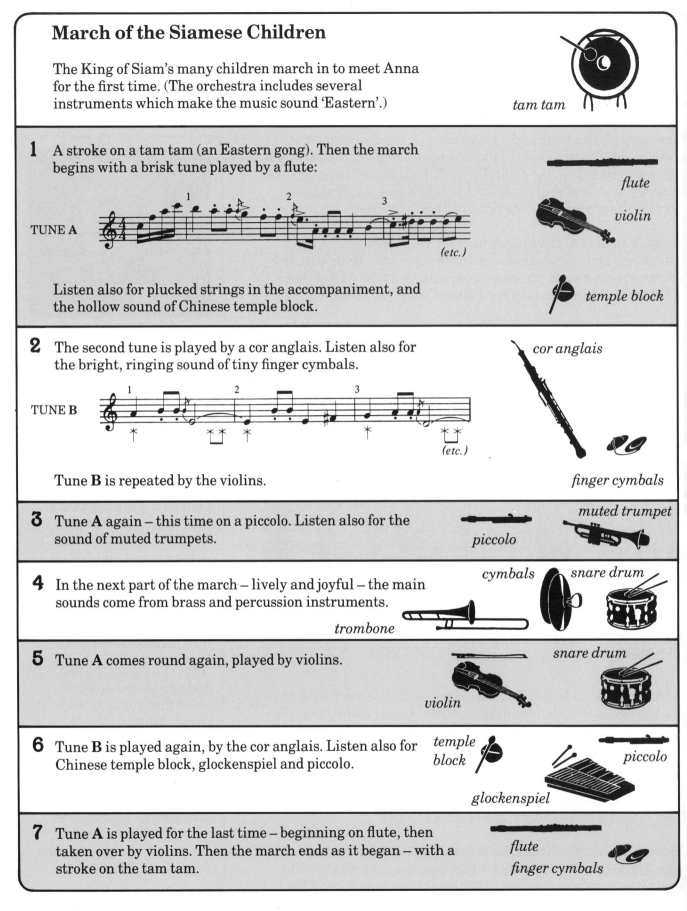

tam tam

1 A stroke on a tam tam (an Eastern gong). Then the march begins with a brisk tune played by a flute:

flute

violin

TUNE A

(etc.)

Listen also for plucked strings in the accompaniment, and the hollow sound of Chinese temple block.

temple block

2 The second tune is played by a cor anglais. Listen also for the bright, ringing sound of tiny finger cymbals.

cor anglais

TUNE B

(etc.)

Tune **B** is repeated by the violins.

finger cymbals

3 Tune **A** again – this time on a piccolo. Listen also for the sound of muted trumpets.

muted trumpet

piccolo

4 In the next part of the march – lively and joyful – the main sounds come from brass and percussion instruments.

cymbals *snare drum*

trombone

5 Tune **A** comes round again, played by violins.

snare drum

violin

6 Tune **B** is played again, by the cor anglais. Listen also for Chinese temple block, glockenspiel and piccolo.

temple block

piccolo

glockenspiel

7 Tune **A** is played for the last time – beginning on flute, then taken over by violins. Then the march ends as it began – with a stroke on the tam tam.

flute

finger cymbals

March of the Siamese Children

A

Listen again to the *March of the Siamese Children* from 'The King and I'. Which instruments do you hear during the March which give the music an 'Eastern' sound?

B

Spelt out in the box below are:

- 4 string instruments
- 3 woodwind instruments
- 5 brass instruments
- 7 percussion instruments

Search, and see how many you can find. (Many of them are heard during the *March of the Siamese Children* – and all of the instruments are mentioned on page 48.)

```
C O R N E T R I A N G L E W X
Y O R B T R O M B O N E B H S
M B A S S U T A M V I O L I N
B O D R U M T A M I P W O P A
A E H A R P I C C O L O C G R
L F L U T E C E L L O O K T E
S H O R N T U B A A Q D R U M
```

Some words (like CORNET) go *across*.
Other words (like CYMBALS) go *down*.

C

1 Listen to a song from *The King and I*. It's called 'I whistle a happy tune'. This song is sung by Anna when she first arrives in Bangkok. It begins with more Eastern-sounding music. Anna is feeling nervous – but she sings the words of her song very clearly.

(Sometimes during the song you will hear tunes whistled, instead of sung.)

2 Listen again to 'I whistle a happy tune'. And each time you hear a tune being whistled – join in, and whistle too.

D

During 'The King and I', Richard Rodgers often makes his music sound 'Eastern'. Now listen to some genuine Eastern music – from the island of Bali, in Indonesia. This music is from a dance-play called 'Barong'. Barong is a mythical creature, a fantastic lion, who guards Bali against evil. In the dance-play he fights against Rangda, Queen of the Witches, who brings darkness, illness and death.

The music is played by a **gamelan**. This is a Balinese orchestra made up mainly of percussion instruments. Among those you will hear are:

xylophones
small cymbals (called *ceng-ceng*)
gongs, of different sizes
metallophones – like the *saron*
gong-chimes – like the *reyong*
double-headed drums – like the *kendang*

You will also hear men imitating the roars of Barong, as he defeats and destroys Rangda, Queen of the Witches.

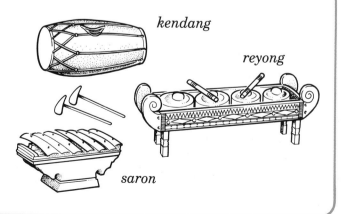

kendang

reyong

saron

¶Instruments of the orchestra

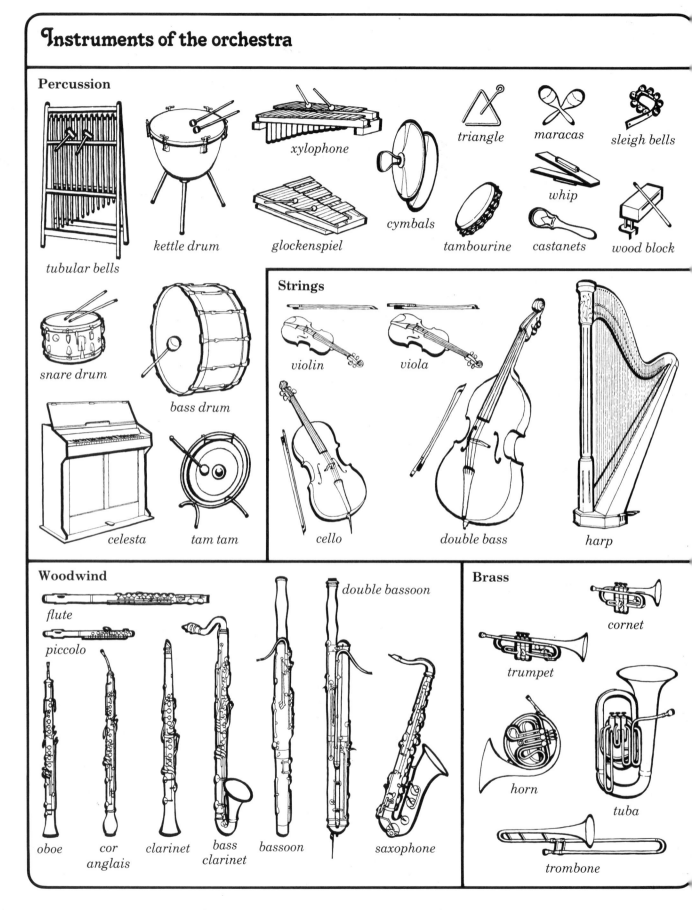

Percussion

tubular bells

kettle drum

xylophone

glockenspiel

cymbals

triangle

maracas

sleigh bells

whip

tambourine

castanets

wood block

snare drum

bass drum

celesta

tam tam

Strings

violin

viola

cello

double bass

harp

Woodwind

flute

piccolo

oboe

cor anglais

clarinet

bass clarinet

double bassoon

bassoon

saxophone

Brass

cornet

trumpet

horn

tuba

trombone